FULL OF
B·E·A·N·S !
Super Healthy Recipes for Kids to Cook Themselves

By the same author
EVELYN FINDLATER'S NATURAL FOODS PRIMER
THORSONS VEGETARIAN FOOD PROCESSOR
EVELYN FINDLATER'S WHOLEFOOD COOKERY COURSE
MAKING YOUR OWN HOME PROTEINS
OFF THE SHELF

FULL OF
B·E·A·N·S !

Super Healthy Recipes for Kids to Cook Themselves

EVELYN FINDLATER

Illustrated by Jill Gibbon

THORSONS PUBLISHING GROUP
Wellingborough, Northamptonshire
—— · ——
Rochester, Vermont

First published 1987

© EVELYN FINDLATER 1987

British Library Cataloguing in Publication Data

Findlater, Evelyn
Full of beans!: super healthy recipes
for kids to cook themselves.
1. Cookery, International
I. Title
641.5   TX725.A1

ISBN 0-7225-1295-3

Printed in Italy by G. Canale and Co SpA, Turin

1 3 5 7 9 10 8 6 4 2

CONTENTS

INTRODUCTION

TO THE BOSS OF THE KITCHEN

In most households there is one person who is usually responsible for buying and preparing the food. To this person I say, 'Let the kids in, and help them to learn an art which is the very basis of our survival.'

We all have to eat to live but feeding a family is hard work. For some, it is a chore to be finished as quickly as possible. If you feel this way, letting helpers into your domain may seem more trouble than it's worth. Teaching is time-consuming and there's bound to be more mess to clear up afterwards! But children can become very good at cooking, so they may take some of the burden off you in the long run.

I have brought up four children, and have certainly not always been the most patient of mums, but I have found with my youngest child who is five and loves to help with cooking and clearing up, that the more I let her into the kitchen, the more peacefully she carries on with her own pursuits at other times.

Children ask lots of questions, and preparing food teaches them about the world they live in. They learn to identify the different ingredients and become familiar with simple practical science as they watch yeast liquids froth, or cakes rising because of the baking powder in them.

I find that teaching young children to cook stops me from taking food for granted. Their curiosity and deep involvement in the process of preparing and cooking, and their obvious joy at seeing their efforts eaten with relish, is refreshing and turns a chore into an exciting happening.

It will take time and patience to begin with, but practice makes perfect and then the children can become useful and enthusiastic helpers doing something they thoroughly enjoy.

WHICH FOODS TO BUY

Today people are more aware than ever before that the best foods are whole natural foods with nothing added to them and nothing taken away. We now know that eating too much sugar, saturated fat, and processed foods which contain very little fibre, can damage our health. Read the labels on the packets and cans in the supermarket, and you will see that, not only is the food inside stripped of most of its goodness but it is often packed with harmful additives to flavour, colour and preserve it. Research has shown that growing children are particularly vulnerable to these additives and the serious effects they can have on our bodies.

The recipes in this book contain fresh, natural ingredients such as wholegrains, nuts and seeds, and fresh fruit and vegetables. Very little sugar and salt is used, and only occasionally is 81% wheatmeal or unbleached white flour used instead of 100% wholemeal flour. If whole natural foods are eaten regularly, it won't hurt to incorporate a few less wholesome ingredients in your cooking from time to time.

I have tested all the recipes on young children and teenagers as well as on adults, with great success all round. You can't fool young cooks easily. They like to see their efforts rewarded with genuine praise and clean plates. I hope this book helps them to choose and use nature's lovely foods to prepare healthy meals that will be enjoyed by all the family.

TO THE YOUNG COOKS

You could not survive without food, but you can make mealtimes more interesting than just eating food because you have to. The recipes in this book will not only feed your body, but will also help to give it strength, energy and health as it grows.

I think that preparing any foods, whether it be a simple cheese on toast or the most carefully planned meal, should give a cook lots of joy because it is a bit like painting a picture or kicking a football into the goal. Choosing and blending colours for a painting is just like mixing ingredients for a recipe, and when you place a carefully prepared meal on the table it can be as exciting as scoring a goal or hanging your picture on the wall for all to see and enjoy.

But cooking can become a bore, like homework, especially for adults who have to do it most of the time. So just remember that Mum, Dad or whoever usually cooks in your house needs a break sometimes.

I hope that this book helps you to give them a real rest from the kitchen. This list of rules sets out the way you should work, whichever recipe you are following.

RULES OF THE KITCHEN

1 Choose your recipe, read it through and make a list of the ingredients you need to buy. A good cook must also learn to shop well and buy only the purest and freshest of ingredients.

2 Wash your hands and wear an apron before preparing any food.

3 If your hair is long, tie it back.

4 Measure all the ingredients and set them out in the order they are going to be used.

5 Make sure that all your pots, pans, bowls, baking trays, dishes or tins are clean and ready to use.

6 Always turn the handles of saucepans or frying pans towards the back of the cooker when frying or boiling.

9

7 Stick sharp knives into a cork when you are not using them, to avoid accidents.

8 Clear up as you go along or you will find that the work surfaces will be full and messy before you have finished preparing.

9 And finally, most important of all, leave the kitchen clean because this encourages willing help with the washing-up afterwards. It also means you might be allowed into the kitchen to cook more often.
Happy cooking!

1. NICE 'N' EASY SAVOURY TUMMY FILLERS

These recipes are all quick and easy to prepare, and tasty and satisfying snacks for hungry tummies.

CRUNCHY COTTAGE CHEESE BUTTIES

Sandwiches are called butties in the North of England. Wholewheat crisps are delicious in sandwiches with your favourite filling. This recipe makes 2 bumper crunchy butties.

Equipment	Ingredients
A vegetable knife	4 slices wholemeal bread
A fork	A little polyunsaturated
A small mixing bowl	margarine
	1 small eating apple, cored and chopped
	4 oz (110g) carton cottage cheese
	1 packet wholewheat crisps

1 Spread the bread with the margarine.

2 Mix the cottage cheese with the chopped apple and the crisps.

3 Divide the mixture equally between the two sandwiches.

11

CHARLIE'S TOASTED SALAD DELIGHTS

Here is my family's favourite five-minute meal. These lovely crunchy toasties were first made by my daughter Charlotte one day when she had to prepare her own lunch in a hurry.

Equipment	Ingredients
A vegetable knife	2 slices wholemeal bread
A cheese grater	A little polyunsaturated margarine
	2 spring onions (or 1 if they are large)
	2 generous tablespoons bean or seed sprouts
	A sprinkling of soya sauce
	6 thin slices of tomato
	4 oz (115g) grated Cheddar cheese

1 Toast the bread on both sides and spread with the margarine.

2 Chop the spring onions and spoon on to the toast.

3 Spread a tablespoon of sprouts on each piece of toast. Sprinkle a very little soya sauce on top.

4 Top with the grated cheese, pressing it gently over the salad ingredients.

5 Cook under a hot grill until golden.

Try these other tasty salad fillings under the cheese:
Shredded cabbage, cucumber slices and thin rings of sweet red pepper;
or Watercress, thinly sliced mushrooms and chopped chives.

WELSH RAREBIT

In very old cook books this hearty snack is sometimes called Welsh Rabbit.
I use milk in this recipe, but in the old days beer was stirred into the melted
cheese instead. It tastes really good so why not try it some time, just for
a change.

Equipment	Ingredients
A medium-sized heavy-based saucepan A wooden spoon A cheese grater	2 slices wholemeal bread A little polyunsaturated margarine for spreading 1 oz (30g) polyunsaturated margarine for sauce ¼ level teaspoon dry mustard powder 2 tablespoons milk ½ teaspoon Holbrooks Worcester sauce 4 oz (115g) grated Cheddar cheese

1 Toast the bread on both sides. Turn out the grill and spread the toast with a little margarine. Keep warm under the grill.

2 Put the margarine, mustard powder, milk, and Worcester sauce in the saucepan and melt on low heat.

3 Stir in the cheese and cook, still on low heat, until the cheese melts.

4 Spoon on to the warm toast and put under a hot grill until golden and bubbling slightly.

13

FLUFFY HERB AND CHEESE OMELETTE

If you are really hungry, you will probably be able to manage the whole of this melt-in-the-mouth omelette on your own! But if you serve it with a salad and perhaps a baked jacket potato, it will fill two hungry tummies.

Equipment
An 8-inch (20cm) frying pan
A medium-sized mixing bowl
An egg whisk
A small vegetable knife
A cheese grater
A palette knife
2 plates, warmed ready to
   serve the omelettes

Ingredients
3 large free range eggs
2 tablespoons cold milk
1 rounded tablespoon fresh
   chopped parsley
½ teaspoon dried mixed
   herbs
A good pinch of sea salt
1 tablespoon corn oil or
   sunflower oil
2 oz (55g) grated Cheddar
   cheese
A pinch of dried herbs to
   garnish

1 Put the eggs, water, parsley, dried herbs, and sea salt into the mixing bowl and whisk for 30 seconds.

2 Heat the oil in the frying pan on moderate heat.

3 When the fat is hot, pour in the egg mixture.

4 Cook until the omelette begins to set round the edges.

5 Sprinkle on the cheese and continue to cook for a further 20 seconds.

6 Cook under a moderate grill until the top is golden brown.

7 Sprinkle on some dried herbs for garnish. Cut the omelette in half and, using the palette knife, ease half on to each of the warm serving plates.

SWEETCORN FRITTERS

Fritters are very easy to make. This recipe uses corn but you can add other vegetables instead. At the end of the recipe, there is a variation for you to experiment with.

Equipment	Ingredients
A frying pan	6 oz (175g) frozen sweetcorn
A small saucepan	3 oz (85g) grated Cheddar cheese
A colander	3 oz (85g) wholemeal flour
A medium-sized mixing bowl	1 oz (30g) soya flour
A fork	1 level teaspoon baking powder
A fish slice	1 large egg
A small vegetable chopping knife	½ teaspoon sea salt
A cheese grater	8 fl oz (225g) milk
A tablespoon	1 small onion (about 2 oz/55g)
Absorbent kitchen paper	Sunflower oil for frying

1 Cook the sweetcorn in a little boiling water, with a pinch of sea salt added, for 3 minutes only. Drain and leave to cool in a colander.

2 Peel the onion and chop it into very small pieces.

3 Put the flours in a mixing bowl with the baking powder and sea salt. Mix together. Make a well in the middle, break in the egg and pour in half the milk. Blend with the fork until smooth. Gradually add the rest of the milk to form a smooth batter.

4 Stir in the onion, the cooled sweetcorn, and the grated cheese. Leave to stand for 10 minutes. Stir before cooking.

5 Heat 2 tablespoons of oil in the frying pan on moderate heat.

6 Use 1 tablespoon of batter for each fritter and make three at a time. Add the 3 spoons of batter to the hot oil, spreading each one gently with the back of the spoon.

7 Fry the fritters until they are golden brown at the edges and bubbling on top.

8 Flick them over, using the fish slice, and cook the other side on a slightly lower heat until golden brown.

9 Drain on kitchen paper and serve immediately.

For a change, try these Vegetable Fritters.

Make the batter in the way described above, and add the onion, with 2 tablespoons of finely chopped red or green pepper and 2 tablespoons of finely chopped mushrooms instead of the sweetcorn. Fry as above.

GRATED POTATO PANCAKES

Feel like a fry-up? Well, make it as healthy as possible using the minimum amount of oil. These crispy pancakes are just the job when you feel like a plate of chips, you only need a few tablespoons of oil so they are better for you. It's like having egg and chips all in one, and it's even tastier.

Equipment	Ingredients
A mixing bowl	3 good size potatoes (about 1 lb/455g)
A small bowl	3 standard eggs
A potato peeler if using very old potatoes	2 tablespoons wholemeal or 81% wheatmeal flour
A grater	1 medium onion (about 4 oz/115g)
An egg whisk	½ teaspoon sea salt
A tablespoon	A little freshly ground black pepper
A frying pan	Sunflower oil for frying
A fish slice	
Absorbent kitchen paper	

1 Scrub the potatoes well. If you are using very old potatoes, you can take off the skin with a potato peeler; otherwise leave it on.

2 Grate the potatoes on the large holes of the grater.

3 Grate the onion on the small holes of the grater. Chop the last little bits if you cannot grate it all.

4 Beat the eggs well.

5 Put the grated potato and onion, flour, salt and eggs into the mixing bowl and stir together.

6 Heat enough oil to just cover the bottom of the pan.

7 Drop tablespoons of the mixture into the pan and fry quickly. When the edges look brown, flip them over with the fish slice and brown the other side. Drain on kitchen paper and serve piping hot with cottage cheese and one of the salads on page 46.

BAKED SCOTCH EGGS

If you like munching through shop-bought Scotch eggs, you will enjoy this recipe even more. Usually, the hard-boiled eggs are covered with a mixture of minced pork meat and cereal. The outside is then coated with orange-tinted crumbs. I prefer to cover the eggs with Granose Sosfry, which is a vegetarian sausage mix and so full of flavour that you don't need to bother with the crumbs.

Equipment
A small saucepan
A small mixing bowl
A rolling pin
A pallette knife
A small baking dish (a pie dish will be perfect)
Foil
Absorbent kitchen paper
A serving dish

Pre-heat the oven at 425°F (220°/Gas Mark 7)

Ingredients
5 oz (140g) Granose Sosfry
8 fl oz (225ml) cold water
4 large eggs
A little wholemeal flour for rolling
2 tablespoons corn oil or sunflower oil
1 tablespoon fresh chopped parsley to garnish

1 Put the eggs in the saucepan, cover with cold water and boil for 10 minutes.

2 When they are cooked, let cold water run into the saucepan for 1 minute, then crack the eggs slightly and the shells will peel off easily. Leave to cool while you prepare the sosfry mixture.

3 Put the sosfry mix in a bowl. Stir in the cold water. Mix well and leave to stand for 5 minutes.

4 Sprinkle flour on a work surface and flour your rolling pin.

5 Divide the mixture in four equal pieces. Roll each one out in a rough circle. Each piece should be slightly smaller than a saucer and not too thin.

6 Ease the circles off the work surface with a palette knife. Put each one in the palm of your hand and place an egg in the centre. Mould the mixture around the egg, pressing it firmly. If it feels a little sticky, dampen your hands before moulding.

7 Place each covered egg in the baking dish. Trickle an equal amount of oil over each egg.

8 Cover the top of the dish with foil and bake in the oven for 25 minutes.

9 Take off the foil, flip the eggs over and bake uncovered for a further 10 minutes, until lightly browned.

10 Drain on kitchen paper.

11 Slice each egg in half and sprinkle on the chopped parsley. Serve hot.

2. SOUPS TO WARM YOUR TOES

The three nourishing soups in this chapter will make a delicious meal for four if served with wholemeal bread or the wheatmeal garlic French loaf on page 59, plus a little cheese and fresh fruit to finish.

TOMATO, LEEK AND POTATO SOUP

It's always better to use fresh vegetables rather than tinned, so when tomatoes are cheap buy ripe, juicy ones for this soup.

Equipment
A medium-sized saucepan
A wooden spoon
A vegetable knife
A potato peeler if using very old potatoes
A measuring jug
A small bowl
A liquidizer or a food processor, or a sieve

Ingredients
1 × 14 oz (395g) can or 1 lb fresh tomatoes
2 medium-sized leeks (about 6 oz/175g when washed and trimmed)
2 medium-sized potatoes (about 12 oz/340g)
1¼ pints (700ml) hot water
1 teaspoon dried basil
1 vegetable stock cube
1 tablespoon tomato purée
2 tablespoons natural yogurt
1 rounded teaspoon arrowroot or wholemeal flour
A little chopped parsley to sprinkle on top

1 If you are using fresh tomatoes, you have to take the skins off. Slit the skin near the stalk end and cut a circle around this point (see diagram). Put the tomatoes into boiling water and leave for 3 minutes. Drain off the water and peel off the skins. Chop into small pieces.

2 Scrub the potatoes. If they are new, leave the skins on; if they are old, peel them very thinly and chop into small pieces.

3 Cut the roots and tough green leaves off the leeks. Slice in half lengthwise and wash well. Chop into small pieces.

4 Put the arrowroot or flour in a small bowl, stir in the yogurt and mix to a smooth paste.

5 Heat the oil in the saucepan on moderate heat. Add the potatoes and cook gently for 3 minutes.

6 Add the leeks and tomatoes and continue to cook for a further 2 minutes.

7 Add the hot water, stock cubes and basil. Bring to the boil and simmer with the lid on for 15 minutes.

8 Spoon a little hot soup liquid into the yogurt and flour paste. Blend until smooth and pour into the soup. Stir well and simmer for 5 minutes.

9 To make the soup smooth, blend half at a time in a liquidizer or food processor, or press through a sieve.

10 Put the soup in a warm serving dish and sprinkle on the chopped parsley.

ZINGY WATERCRESS SOUP

Watercress is cheap and full of goodness. It tastes great cooked in soup or chopped raw in salads. This plant grows by streams all over the countryside, but unfortunately it is not safe to pick it yourself because it is often infested with liver flukes, which can cause illness and even death. If you have a garden, you can grow watercress quite easily by following the instructions on the seed packet. I have also grown it in a window box with great success. The most important thing to remember is to water it every day so that the soil stays swampy.

Equipment	Ingredients
A medium-sized saucepan	1 oz (30g) polyunsaturated
A vegetable knife	margarine
A potato peeler if using old	1 tablespoon sunflower oil
potatoes	1 lb (455g) potatoes
A liquidizer or a food	1 onion (about 6 oz/175g
processor	when peeled)
A warmed serving dish	2 bunches fresh green
	watercress
	2 pints (1.1 litres) boiling water
	1½ vegetable stock cubes
	A small carton natural yogurt
	A little freshly ground black
	pepper
	1 tablespoon fresh chopped
	parsley to sprinkle on top

1 Scrub the potatoes and peel thinly if very old; otherwise leave the skins on. Chop into small chunks.

2 Chop the onion.

3 Cut the stems off the watercress and chop them. Put the leaves to one side.

4 Heat the oil and margarine in the saucepan.

5 Fry the potato, onion and watercress stems for 10 minutes on low heat with the lid on the pan.

6 Add the water, stock cubes and watercress leaves and simmer with the lid on for a further 10 minutes.

7 Purée in the liquidizer or food processor.

8 Return to the heat but do not boil.

9 Take off the heat and stir in the yogurt and a little black pepper.

10 Pour into a warm serving dish and sprinkle on the chopped parsley. This is a real treat served with French bread and cheese.

WINTER WARMING LENTIL BROTH

This is a filling and nourishing soup. It is delicious whether served chunky or smooth.

Equipment
A large heavy-based saucepan
A sieve
A vegetable knife
A wooden spoon
A liquidizer or a food processor if you want a smooth-textured soup

Ingredients
1 large onion (about 8 oz (225g)
2 medium-sized carrots
2 sticks celery
1 large clove garlic
1 teaspoon ground coriander (optional)
4 oz (115g) split red lentils
1½ pints (850ml) hot water
1 rounded tablespoon tomato purée
1 vegetable stock cube
1 large bay leaf
1 tablespoon fresh chopped parsley or 1 teaspoon dried parsley
1 tablespoon lemon juice
2 tablespoons Shoyu (soya sauce)

1 Wash the lentils and leave them to drain in a sieve.

2 Peel and chop the onion. Scrape and dice carrots. Wash the celery and chop it into small pieces. Peel the garlic and crush or chop it very finely.

3 Heat the oil in the saucepan and add the chopped vegetables. Cook on gentle heat for 3 minutes.

4 Stir in the coriander powder and drained lentils and cook, stirring all the time, for 1 minute

5 Pour in the hot water, stock cube and bay leaf. Bring to the boil. Turn down the heat. Stir well. Put the lid on and simmer for 45 minutes.

6 Finally, stir in the lemon juice and soya sauce.

Serve hot and chunky, or blend, half at a time, in a liquidizer or food processor until smooth.

Babies over six months old love this soup. Press a portion through a sieve and mix it with a little mashed potato or baby cereal.

3. HOT MAIN DISHES

NUTMEAT BALLS

This is delicious with pasta and Italian tomato sauce. Liquidizing the sauce to a smooth consistency will give it a rich full flavour which goes really well with these nutmeat balls. Serves 6.

Equipment	Ingredients
A liquidizer or a food processor, or a sieve A mixing bowl A medium-sized saucepan (for the sauce) A non-stick frying pan Absorbent kitchen paper A warm ovenproof dish	1 quantity of Italian tomato sauce (see recipe on page 30) 8 oz (225g) mixed nuts and seeds (cashews, hazels, and sunflower seeds) 115g (4 oz) wholemeal breadcrumbs 1 medium onion (4 oz/115g) 1 tablespoon Shoyu (soya sauce) 1 tablespoon sunflower oil 1 large egg A few sprigs of parsley 2 tablespoons sunflower oil for frying

1 Purée the Italian tomato sauce for a few seconds until smooth.

2 Grind the nuts and seeds until they are like fine breadcrumbs (but not too powdery).

3 Chop the onion into very small pieces. Chop the parsley.

4 Put the ground nuts, breadcrumbs, chopped onion, soya sauce, 1 tablespoon sunflower oil, egg, and parsley into the mixing bowl. Mix well and mould together with your hands.

5 Make 24 nutmeat balls from the mixture.

6 Heat 2 tablespoons oil in the frying pan and fry the nutmeat balls on medium heat, turning them so that they brown lightly on all sides. Drain on kitchen paper.

7 Gently heat the puréed sauce.

8 Place the cooked nutmeat balls in a warm ovenproof dish and pour the hot sauce over them. Keep them warm in a cool oven while you prepare your pasta. Sprinkle with a little grated cheese if you like.

ITALIAN TOMATO SAUCE WITH WHOLEMEAL PASTA

This simple and delicious sauce can be served with lots of dishes. With the Nutmeat Balls (page 28) and the recipes on the next pages, you have four scrumptious ways in which you can use it to make a meal for 4 people.

For the Sauce

Equipment	Ingredients
A medium-sized heavy-based saucepan	1 onion (about 6 oz/175g)
A vegetable knife	1 clove garlic
A wooden spoon	2 sticks celery
	2 tablespoons corn oil or olive oil
	1 small green pepper
	A few sprigs of parsley
	1 teaspoon dried basil
	1 bay leaf
	1×14 oz (395g) can of tomatoes
	1 tablespoon tomato purée
	¼ teaspoon sea salt
	2 teaspoons lemon juice

1 Peel the onion and chop it into small pieces.

2 Peel the garlic and crush it or chop it into tiny pieces.

3 Wash the celery and chop it into small pieces.

4 Heat the oil in the saucepan. Fry the onion, garlic and celery for 10 minutes on low heat with the lid on the pan.

5 De-seed the green pepper and chop it into small pieces. Chop the parsley.

6 Add the green pepper, parsley, basil and bay leaf to the onion mixture and fry for a further 3 minutes.

7 Chop the tomatoes roughly and add these, with the purée and lemon juice, to the other ingredients. Cook on low heat for 20 minutes with the lid on the pan. Your sauce is now ready.

TO COOK SPAGHETTI

Spaghetti is a pasta. Pasta is made in all sorts of shapes and sizes and its main ingredient is either white durum semolina flour or wholewheat flour. Wholemeal pasta is far better for you because it contains all the vitamins, minerals and fibre of the whole grain. You can use pasta twirls, pasta shells, spaghetti rings or tagliatelle for this recipe, instead of spaghetti. Tagiatelle is long thin strips of pasta which is sometimes green because spinach is added to the flour. Then it is called tagiatelle verdi.

Equipment	Ingredients
A large saucepan A colander	8 oz (225g) wholewheat spaghetti or other wholewheat pasta 1 level teaspoon sea salt 1 tablespoon corn oil or sunflower oil (this stops the pasta from sticking together) Grated cheese to sprinkle on top of the sauce

1 Bring about 2 pints (1.1 litres) of water to the boil.

2 Add the salt and oil, then gradually ease in the spaghetti.

3 Stir the pasta around, separating the strands. Keep the water bubbling and cook without a lid for 15 minutes, or the time it states on the packet.

4 Drain in a colander and serve immediately, topped with the Italian tomato sauce and a little grated cheese. Serves 4.

QUICKIE PIZZA

Pizza dough is usually made with yeast which means that you have to wait ages for it to rise. The Pizza base in this recipe only takes 5 minutes to prepare, and then you can make a tasty topping of Italian tomato sauce (see page 30), grated cheese and pumpkin seeds. I use the seeds instead of olives because most children do not like the salty taste of olives.

Equipment
A medium-sized mixing bowl
A jug
A rolling pin
A large pizza tray (12 inches/30cm), well oiled
(Using a larger tray than the size of the pizza prevents the sauce and melting cheese from dripping over the edge and messing up the oven.)

Pre-heat the oven at 400°F (200°C/Gas Mark 6)

Ingredients

For the pizza base
6 oz (175g) wholemeal flour
1 rounded teaspoon baking powder
2 tablespoons sesame seeds
½ tablespoon sea salt
2 tablespoons corn oil or olive oil
2 tablespoons water
2 tablespoons natural yogurt

For the topping
1 quantity of Italian tomato sauce (see recipe on page 30)
5 oz (150g) grated cheese
1 oz (30g) pumpkin seeds
A pinch of dried mixed herbs

1 Make the sauce and keep it hot.

2 Put the flour, seeds and salt into a bowl. Mix together and pour in the oil, water and yogurt.

3 Form into a soft dough with your hands.

4 On a lightly-floured surface, roll the dough out to make a 9-inch (23cm) circle.

5 Lift the dough on to the rolling pin and lay it in the centre of the pizza tray.

6 Spoon on the tomato sauce. Top with the cheese, pumpkin seeds and herbs.

7 Bake in the oven for 25 minutes until the top is golden brown. Let the pizza stand for 5 minutes before cutting.

RISOTTO WITH TOASTED CASHEW NUTS

You will see that Surinam brown rice is used in this recipe. This is the lightest and quickest to cook of all the varieties of brown rice I have tried. Brown rice is far better for you than white rice because it contains all the goodness of the wholegrain. It also has much more flavour than white rice.

Equipment
A medium-sized heavy-based saucepan with a light lid
A medium-sized saucepan (for the sauce)
A sieve
A colander
A baking tray
A serving bowl
A grinder for nuts

Pre-heat the oven to 325°F (160°C/Gas Mark 3)

Ingredients
1 quantity of Italian tomato sauce (see recipe on page 30)
8 oz (225g) Surinam long-grain brown rice
1 level teaspoon sea salt
4 oz (115g) cashew nuts
A pinch of sea salt

1 Put the rice on a flat baking tray and pick out the dark brown grains which still have the tough husks on. You will only find about a teaspoonful.

2 Put the rice in a sieve and wash it by running cold water through the grains for half a minute. Then put the washed rice into the saucepan with 2 cups of water and a pinch of salt. Bring to the boil, turn the heat down to simmer, cover the pan and cook for 25 minutes. Do not stir the rice during cooking time.

3 While the rice is cooking, put the nuts on a baking tray and toast them in the oven for 15 minutes, then grind them coarsely adding a good pinch of salt.

4 When the rice is cooked, heat the tomato sauce. Place the cooked rice in a serving bowl. Stir in the tomato sauce with a fork and sprinkle on the roughly-ground cashew nuts.

CHINESE FRIED RICE

This tasty mixture of rice, almonds and peas is another family favourite. Not only does it taste great, but once you get the hang of cooking rice well, it's simple to prepare too. Spreading the hot rice out on a tray to let off steam is a method used in China and Japan — it stops the rice sticking together in gluey lumps and makes it easier to fry. If you have some chopsticks which never seem to leave the kitchen drawer, you could try them out on this dish! You'll be surprised how easy they are to use once you have had a bit of practice.

Equipment	Ingredients
A baking tray	8 oz (225g) Surinam long-grain brown rice, cooked as on page 34
A saucepan	1 large onion (8 oz/225g)
A frying pan	3 oz (85g) almonds
A vegetable knife	2 tablespoons sunflower oil
A wooden spoon	4 oz (115g) frozen peas
	1 tablespoons Shoyu (soya sauce)
	2 tablespoons lemon juice

1 When the rice is cooked, spread it out on a large flat baking tray to let the steam off.

2 Put the almonds in a little boiling water and leave for 3 minutes then pop the skins off.

3 Cook the peas in lightly-salted boiling water for just 3 minutes. Drain.

4 Skin and chop the onion and fry it in the oil for 10 minutes with the lid on the pan. Stir in the almonds, peas and the soya sauce.

5 Stir in the rice, coating it thoroughly with the onions and sauce. Fry gently for 1 minute until heated right through.

NUTTY STUFFED POTATOES

I don't know anyone who would say 'no' to a baked jacket potato. They are lovely with a little butter or margarine, or slit open and topped with dollops of cottage cheese. They can also be stuffed in many exciting and nourishing ways. Try this very popular recipe — it will take a little time to prepare but it is well worth the effort.

Equipment	Ingredients
A saucer	4 good-sized potatoes (about 6 oz/175g each)
A vegetable knife	
A fork	2 teaspoons sunflower oil or corn oil
A cheese grater	
A mixing bowl	3 oz (85g) sunflower seeds
A potato masher	3 tablespoons fresh chopped parsley
A baking tray	
	3 spring onions
	2 rounded tablespoons natural yogurt
	1 oz (30g) polyunsaturated margarine
	A little sea salt and black pepper
Pre-heat the oven to 400°F (200°C/Gas Mark 6)	4 oz (115g) grated Cheddar cheese grated

1 Scrub the potatoes and cut out any bad bits.

2 Put the oil in a saucer and roll each potato in it. (This stops the skins from drying out too much.) Prick the potatoes all over with a fork, and bake them in the oven for 50-60 minutes.

3 Test if they are cooked by pushing a skewer or knife through the centre.

4 Grind the seeds until they look like fine breadcrumbs.

5 Chop the spring onions into tiny pieces, including the green ends of stems as well as the white tops.

6 When the potatoes are ready, take them out of the oven but leave the oven on. Cut the potatoes in half lengthwise and scoop out the pulp.

7 Place the pulp in a bowl with the yogurt, margarine, ground seeds, spring onions, parsley and half the cheese. Mash the mixture with the potato masher or a fork. Taste and add a little sea salt and pepper if you like.

8 Spoon this mixture into the potato skins. Sprinkle on the rest of the grated cheese. Put the potatoes on a baking tray and bake in the oven for 15 minutes until they are golden-brown on top. Serve with a fresh salad.

SAVOURY MILLET PATTIES

Millet is a tasty and nourishing grain and I don't see why the birds should be the only ones to enjoy it. It is probably best to try this recipe when an adult can spare the time to help you toast and cook the millet because getting the texture right can be a bit tricky until you have had some practice. When cooked, the millet should have absorbed all the cooking water and have a soft texture that is easy to mould into patties.

Equipment	Ingredients
A medium-sized heavy-based saucepan	1 tablespoon corn oil or sunflower oil
A wooden spoon	8 oz (225g) wholegrain millet
A vegetable knife	1 pint (560ml) boiling water
A non-stick frying pan with lid	½ teaspoon sea salt
A small bowl	1 onion (about 6 oz/140g)
An egg whisk	1 tablespoon corn oil or sunflower oil
A pastry brush	1 teaspoon dried sage and 1 teaspoon dried marjoram
Absorbent kitchen paper	1 egg to bind
	1 egg to coat
	2 tablespoons corn oil for frying

1 Heat 1 tablespoon oil in the saucepan and toast the millet on moderate heat, stirring constantly, for 3 minutes. Take it off the heat.

2 Pour in the boiling water and the sea salt and simmer on low heat, with the lid on the pan, for 25 minutes.

3 Peel the onion and chop it into very small pieces.

4 Heat 1 tablespoon oil in the frying pan and fry the onion on low heat, with the lid on the pan, for 10 minutes.

5 Stir in the dried herbs. Take the pan off the heat.

6 When the millet is cooked, take it off the heat and stir in the onion mixture and grated cheese. Break the egg into the mixture, and mould it together well with your hands.

7 Whisk the other egg in the small bowl.

8 Form the slightly cooled millet mixture into ten round burger shapes, each about ½ inch thick.

9 Use the pastry brush to lightly coat the burgers with beaten egg. This helps to stop the burgers breaking up.

10 Heat 2 tablespoons oil in the frying pan and fry the millet burgers on medium heat for 2 minutes on each side. Drain on kitchen paper.

BOSTON BAKED BEANS

These keep well for a few days in the fridge. Serve them on wholemeal toast for a quick satisfying snack or with baked jacket potatoes and salad for a very wholesome meal.

Equipment	Ingredients
A mixing bowl	8 oz (225g) haricot beans
A colander	2 tablespoons tomato purée
A medium-sized saucepan	1 level tablespoon Barbados sugar
A casserole dish with a lid	1 level tablespoon molasses
	½ teaspoon dry mustard powder
	½ pint (275ml) hot water
	1 teaspoon Holbrook's Worcester sauce
	1 vegetable stock cube
	1 bay leaf
	½ teaspoon dried mixed herbs

1 Soak the beans overnight, changing the water once.

2 Drain, rinse in a colander and put into the saucepan. Add 2 pints (1.1 litres) cold water, bring to the boil, then simmer with the lid on for about 1¼-1½ hours, until the beans are soft but not mushy. Do not add salt or the beans will stay hard.

3 Drain the cooked beans, put them into the casserole dish and add all the other ingredients.

4 Cover and bake in the oven at 300°F (150°C/Gas Mark2) for 2 hours.

WHITE SAUCE

This sauce can be used in many dishes such as cauliflower cheese (see the next recipe) and macaroni cheese. If you fry a small onion in a little oil for 5 minutes before heating the milk, you will have an onion sauce which is delicious poured over your favourite rissoles. I make my sauce with a mixture of unbleached white flour and gram flour. Gram flour is made from powdered chick peas and adds a lovely flavour to sauce and batter mixtures.

Equipment	Ingredients
A measuring jug	1 pint (560ml) milk
A medium-sized heavy-based saucepan	1½ oz (45g) unbleached white flour
A medium-sized mixing bowl	1 oz (30g) gram flour
A fork	½ level teaspoon sea salt
A sieve	A good pinch of ground nutmeg
A wooden spoon	¼ teaspoon mustard powder

1 Heat ¾ pint (425ml) of the milk in the saucepan.

2 Sieve the flours, salt, nutmeg, and mustard powder into the bowl and blend with the remaining cold milk to a smooth paste with no lumps in it. Gradually pour in the hot milk, stirring briskly all the time.

3 Pour the mixture back into the saucepan and cook on moderate heat, stirring all the time. When it is bubbling, turn down the heat and cook gently for 1 minute. Your sauce should be thick and smooth.

CREAMY CAULIFLOWER CHEESE

If you have mastered the simple art of making the delicious white sauce on page 41, this recipe will be very easy for you to tackle. It makes enough for three people.

Equipment
A medium-sized saucepan
A colander which fits snug on top of the saucepan
An ovenproof dish
A vegetable knife

Pre-heat the oven to 375°F (190°C/Gas Mark 5)

Ingredients
1 good-sized cauliflower
2 tablespoons finely chopped parsley
5 oz (140g) grated cheese
1 quantity of white sauce (see recipe on page 41)

1 Trim the leaves off the cauliflower. Wash it well and break into florets.

2 Half-fill the saucepan with water and place the colander on top. Bring the water to the boil.

3 Put the cauliflower florets into the colander, cover with the saucepan lid and steam for 7 minutes.

4 Put the cooked florets into the ovenproof dish.

5 Stir 3 oz (85g) of the cheese and most of the parsley into the white sauce and pour this over the cauliflower. Sprinkle the rest of the cheese on top.

6 Bake in the oven for 15 minutes.

SHORTCRUST WHOLEMEAL PASTRY

I've heard lots of people, even really good cooks, say that making good pastry with wholemeal flour is very difficult. Well, it's not. The most important things to remember are to measure your ingredients out carefully, add the right amount of cold water and chill the dough in the fridge before rolling it out. Most recipes for making pastry tell you to rub the fat into the flour but I get best results by using the creaming method described in this recipe.

Equipment
A mixing bowl
A wooden spoon
A polythene bag

Ingredients
3 oz (85g) polyunsaturated
   margarine
2 tablespoons and 2
   teaspoons cold water
6 oz (170g) wholemeal flour
   (you can buy fine-milled
   wholemeal pastry flour)
¼ teaspoon sea salt

1 Put the margarine, water, sea salt and 2 tablespoons of the flour into the mixing bowl and cream together with a wooden spoon until smooth.

2 Gradually add the remaining flour, 2 tablespoons at a time, stirring with the spoon until the mixture stiffens. Then use your hands to mould it into a soft dough.

3 Knead for 1 minute, then put the pastry into the polythene bag. Chill in the fridge for 10 minutes.

Your pastry is now ready to roll out.

CRISPY POTATO AND LEEK FLAN

The filling for this flan is very simple to make and is a real winner with all who have tasted it. It's just the job if you have lots of people to feed because you can cut eight good-sized portions from a flan of this size. It tastes delicious hot or cold.

Equipment	Ingredients
A 10 inch (25cm) flan dish	1 quantity of shortcrust pastry
A rolling pin	(see recipe on page 43)
A pallet knife	1 large potato (about
A fork	6 oz/175g)
A vegetable knife	1 good-sized leek (about
A wooden spoon	5 oz/140g) when trimmed)
A non-stick frying pan	2 tablespoons sunflower oil
An egg whisk	1 teaspoon mixed dried herbs
A medium-sized bowl	1 bay leaf
	4 eggs
	2 rounded tablespoons natural
	yogurt
	7 fl oz (200ml) milk
	¼ teaspoon sea salt
Pre-heat the oven to 375°F	¼ teaspoon ground nutmeg
(190°C/GAs Mark 5)	3 oz (85g) grated cheese

1 Grease the flan dish.

2 Roll out the pastry on a lightly floured surface.

3 Ease the pastry from the surface with a pallet knife and curl one edge over the rolling pin. Lift the pastry on to the flan dish.

4 Gently press into the bottom and sides of the dish, and trim off the edges.

5 Prick the base with the fork and bake in the centre of the oven for 10 minutes, leave to cool.

6 Scrub the potato and cut out any bad bits. Chop it into small chunks.

7 Heat the oil in a pan and fry the potatoes for 7 minutes with the lid on the pan.

8 Trim the leek, taking off the tough green parts only (some of the green is tender enough so don't cut it all off).

9 Slice down the centre of the leek lengthwise, and wash holding the leaves together.

10 Cut the leek into very small pieces.

11 Sprinkle the leek pieces, herbs and bay leaf on top of the fried potato and continue to fry with the lid on for a further 4 minutes. Allow to cool.

12 Whisk the eggs, yogurt, milk, sea salt, and nutmeg together in a bowl.

13 Spoon the potato and leek mixture into the pastry case, pour over the egg mixture and sprinkle on the grated cheese.

14 Bake in the centre of the oven for 45 minutes, leave to stand for 5 minutes before cutting.

4. SALADS

Raw fresh vegetables and fruit are just about the best foods you can eat. They are packed with vitamins, minerals and fibre, all of which are very important if you want a fit and healthy body. It's a good thing to eat at least one salad every day so, to save time, make a jar full of salad dressing at the beginning of the week and store it in the fridge. Then when you want a salad all you have to do is chop a few salad ingredients, pour over a little dressing and your meal's ready. Always dress the salad as soon as possible after chopping the vegetables because the vitamin C in them is quickly lost when it is exposed to the air.

Salads are even better if you grow some of your own ingredients. Why not try some bean sprouts to start with? You need no garden, no greenhouse, no window boxes, and no earth. All you have to do is water a few seeds daily and you can have bean or seed sprouts any time you like.

The most popular bean sprouts are grown from the small green mung bean, and these are very cheap to buy. But you can sprout many other beans and seeds quite easily, using the method described here.

CRISP LETTUCE, ORANGE AND ALFALFA SEED SALAD

You can use Chinese leaf, Iceberg or Webb's lettuce. All of these are crisp and easy to shred.

If you are using Chinese leaf, which are usually quite big, it is best to cut off what you need lengthwise (see diagram) because the base is very crisp and cabbage-like and the top is softer and more like lettuce. Put the rest in a polythene bag and keep it in the fridge.

<table>
<tr><td>

Equipment
A vegetable knife
A fork
A serving bowl
Absorbent kitchen paper

</td><td>

Ingredients
3 tablespoons salad dressing
    (see page 51)
8 oz (225g) Chinese leaf,
    Iceberg or Webb's lettuce
2 oranges
2 oz (55g) sprouted alfalfa
    seeds (or 1 punnet of
    mustard cress)
4-inch (10cm) piece of
    cucumber

</td></tr>
</table>

1 Wash the lettuce, keeping the leaves together. Dry by patting it with kitchen paper.

2 Shred in very thin strips. Put in a serving bowl.

3 Cut the cucumber lengthwise into six sticks, then cut the sticks into small chunks. Stir them into the shredded lettuce.

4 Add the sprouted alfalfa. (If you are using cress, cut it off from the roots and wash it well before adding to the salad.)

5 Peel the oranges, taking off as much pith (white part) as possible.

6 Cut the orange into small pieces and add to the salad.

7 Pour over the dressing and stir with a fork to coat all the ingredients.

47

GROWING MUNG BEAN SPROUTS

(For 8 oz/225g) sprouted beans)

Equipment	Ingredients
A 1¾-pint (1-litre) wide-rimmed glass jar A sieve A 10-inch (25cm) square piece of clean muslin or net curtain A thick elastic band A polythene bag	2 oz (55g) mung beans

1 Carefully pick over the beans, taking out split or crinkled ones and any small stones.

2 Put the beans in a sieve and wash them well.

3 Soak the beans in cold water overnight (about 12 hours).

4 Drain and rinse the beans and put them in the clean jar. Cover the rim with the muslin or net curtain material and secure with the elastic band.

5 Put the jar in a warm place 60°-65°F/15°-18°C in the kitchen. Do not put it in direct sunlight. (The airing cupboard is ideal for the first 3 days, then you can put it in a kitchen cupboard for 2 days — but be careful not to forget all about it!)

6 Rinse the beans 3 times a day by pouring ½ pint (275ml) of water through the muslin cloth. Roll the jar so that all the beans get wet, then carefully pour the water out through the muslin.

7 Do this for 5 days. Your sprouts will then be ready.

8 Put the sprouts in a polythene bag and keep them in the fridge. They will keep fresh for 3 days.

GROWING ALFALFA
SEED SPROUTS

These tiny seeds are fully of goodness. When sprouted, the small shoots are light, crisp and great in salads and sandwiches.

Equipment	Ingredients
A 1¾-pint (1-litre) wide-rimmed glass jar	2 oz (55g) alfalfa seeds
A sieve	
A 10-inch (25cm) square piece of clean muslin or net curtain	
A thick elastic band	
A polythene bag	

1 Put the seeds in the sieve and rinse them with cold water.

2 Soak the seeds in cold water for 6 hours or overnight.

3 Follow the directions for mung bean sprouts (page 48) rinsing 3 times a day. Alfalfa seeds need 6 days watering before the sprouts are ready to eat.

4 When they are ready, put them in a polythene bag and store them in the fridge. They will stay fresh for 3 days.

CRUNCHY BEAN SPROUT SALAD

Equipment
A vegetable knife
A grater
A serving bowl
Absorbent kitchen paper

Ingredients
8 oz (225g) mung bean sprouts
1 good-sized carrot
2 spring onions, or a small
    bunch of chives
½ small red or green pepper

1 Wash the bean sprouts and pat them dry with kitchen paper.

2 Wash and scrape the carrot. Slice it in very thin rings, using a vegetable knife or the slicing slit on a grater (see diagram).

3 Chop the spring onions or chives into tiny pieces. Use the green as well as the white parts of the spring onions.

4 Chop the red or green pepper, making sure that you remove all the seeds and white flesh.

5 Mix all the ingredients in a serving bowl and pour over 2 tablespoons of salad dressing (see the next recipe).

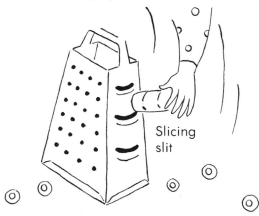

Slicing
slit

SALAD DRESSING

Equipment
- A jam or honey screw-top jar (make sure it is really clean)
- A lemon squeezer

Ingredients
- 3 tablespoons sunflower, corn or olive oil
- 1 tablespoon freshly squeezed lemon juice
- 2 teaspoons freshly squeezed orange or satsuma juice
- ¼ teaspoon sea salt
- ¼ teaspoon mustard powder (optional)
- ½ teaspoon clear honey (optional)
- 1 small clove garlic, peeled and crushed

Put all the ingredients into the clean jar, shake well and store in the fridge until needed. Make double this quantity to use as you need it. It will store well for at least a week.

LEMON MAYONNAISE

I think that I have found the secret for never-fail mayonnaise. You can make this just as easily with an egg whisk or a liquidizer or food processor. If you are using an egg whisk, you will need a helper to pour the oil. The result, whether you use the hand or machine method is a lovely, smooth, thickish salad cream which will last for at least 2 weeks in a screw-top jar in the fridge. My secret is never to add the lemon juice until the mixture is thick. The oil and egg thicken much quicker if they are beaten together without the juice. Adding the juice last also seems to prevent curdling.

Equipment	Ingredients
A liquidizer or a food processor *or* an egg whisk, a mixing bowl and a helping hand A lemon squeezer	1 large egg ½ teaspoon sea salt ½ teaspoon made mustard or dry mustard power 8 fl oz (225ml) sunflower oil or corn oil 2 tablespoons freshly squeezed lemon juice

Machine method

1 Put the egg, sea salt, mustard and 2 tablespoons of the oil into the liquidizer. Process on medium speed for 30 seconds.

2 Pour the rest of the oil in a steady stream into the egg mixture, keeping the machine on all the time. The mixture will become quite thick when you have finished pouring.

3 Pour in the lemon juice and blend a further 10 seconds.

Hand Method

1 Break the egg into the mixing bowl. Add the sea salt, mustard, and 2 tablespoons of the oil.

2 Whisk vigorously for 1 minute.

3 Still whisking, get your helper to pour the rest of the oil into the egg mixture in a very thin stream. The mixture will thicken near the end of pouring.

4 Pour in the lemon juice, still whisking vigorously.

POTATO SALAD

You can try out your home-made mayonnaise in this delightful salad mix. If you haven't the time to make your own mayonnaise, buy one which has no added preservatives or colouring.

Equipment	Ingredients
A medium-sized saucepan	1 lb (455g) potatoes
A colander which fits snugly into the rim of the saucepan	3 tender inside sticks of celery
	1 tablespoons very finely chopped onion
A potato peeler, if using very old potatoes	4 oz (115g) each of frozen peas and sweetcorn
A vegetable knife	2 tablespoons very finely chopped parsley
A serving bowl	

1 Wash the potatoes. If they are new, leave the skins on; if they are old, scrub them and peel a very thin skin off with the potato peeler.

2 Cut the potatoes in four lengthwise. Half-fill the saucepan with water and put the colander on top. Put the cut potatoes into the colander, cover with the saucepan lid, bring the water to the boil, turn down to simmer and leave to steam for 20 minutes. Allow the potatoes to cool slightly before cutting them into small chunks.

3 Cook the peas and sweetcorn in lightly salted water for 3 minutes only. Drain.

4 Wash the celery and chop it into small pieces.

5 Put the potatoes, peas, corn, celery, onion, and parsley into a serving bowl and stir in 4 or more tablespoons of mayonnaise. (Stir in the mayonnaise while the ingredients are still warm. Sprinkle with parsley.

WHITE CABBAGE AND ROASTED CASHEW NUT SALAD

White cabbage is cheap to buy and lasts for ages in the fridge. Get a big one and cut quarters off lengthwise when you feel like making a crunchy salad. Store the rest in a polythene bag in the bottom of the fridge. In this recipe I suggest dressing the salad with mayonnaise, but it tastes just as good with salad dressing (page 51).

Equipment	Ingredients
A baking tray	2 oz (55g) cashew nuts
A serving bowl	1 teaspoon sunflower oil
A vegetable knife	A good pinch of sea salt
A small mixing bowl	12 oz (340g) white cabbage
	1 good-sized eating apple (red looks good)
	1 tablespoon very finely chopped onion
	2 oz (55g) sultanas or raisins
	2 tablespoons finely chopped parsley
	5 tablespoons lemon mayonnaise (see page 52)
Pre-heat the oven to 325°F (160°C/Gas Mark 3)	3 tablespoons plain yogurt

1 Put the nuts on the baking tray. Rub in the oil and sea salt. Roast in the oven for 15 minutes. Allow to cool.

2 Wash the cabbage and shred it as thinly as possible.

3 Core the apple and chop it into very small chunks (leave the skins on).

4 When the nuts are cool, put them into the serving bowl and stir in the cabbage, apple, onion, sultanas or raisins, and parsley.

5 In the small mixing bowl, stir yogurt and mayonnaise together.

6 Stir this into the salad ingredients and keep it cool until you are ready to serve it.

5. HOME-BAKED BREAD AND CAKES

There is nothing better then the smell of freshly-baked bread, and not many of us would refuse a slice of home-made cake or fruit pie. Unlike many breads and cakes, these home-bakes are not only delicious but they are so full of wholesome ingredients that they are good for you too!

Most of the recipes include wholemeal flour with the exception of baps, cheese scones and sweet shortcrust pastry, where 81% wheatmeal flour is used to obtain a lighter mixture. But, as I have said before, a few indulgences won't hurt if you eat well most of the time.

WHEATMEAL BAPS

This mixture will also make delicious French loaves. You can fill baps or chunks of French bread with salad and other ingredients for picnics and packed lunches. The recipe makes twelve baps or three French loaves.

Equipment
A large mixing bowl
1 2-pint (1¼-litre) measuring jug
A small bowl
A fork
A large oiled polythene bag
2 baking trays, greased and lightly floured
A pastry brush
2 large polythene bags, opened and greased, to cover the rising baps
A wire rack

Ingredients
1½ lb (680g) 81% wheatmeal plain flour
4 oz (115g) soya flour
1 teaspoon sea salt
½ pint (275ml) warm water
¼ pint (140ml) warm milk
1 level tablespoon dried yeast
1 dessertspoon malt extract
1 egg
1 oz (30g) sesame seeds

1 Mix the wheatmeal flour, soya flour and sea salt in the bowl.

2 Measure the warm water and the milk in the jug. Stir in the yeast and the malt, and mix well.

3 Cover the yeast liquid with a small plate and leave to froth in a warm place for about 7 minutes.

4 Whisk the egg.

5 When the yeast liquid is ready, make a well in the middle of the flour mixture and pour it in. Add the egg.

6 Mix all the ingredients together with your hands and form into a soft dough.

7 Put the dough on a lightly-floured surface and knead for 7 minutes. If the dough is sticky, flour your hands as you knead.

8 Put the dough into the greased polythene bag, wrap it in a warm towel and leave to rise in a warm kitchen for about 40 minutes or until it has doubled in size.

9 Pre-heat the oven to 425°F (220°C/Gas Mark 7).

10 Take out the dough and knead it for 2 minutes.

11 Break the dough into twelve equal pieces and put them back into the polythene bag until you need them, otherwise they will dry out.

12 Roll each piece of dough into a ball and place six on each baking tray with plenty of space between them.

13 Cover each tray with an opened and greased polythene bag and leave to rise in a warm place until the baps have doubled in size.

14 Brush the tops of the baps with a little warm water and sprinkle on the sesame seeds.

15 Put the trays on to two shelves in the oven, one just above and one just below the centre. Bake for 18 minutes, changing the trays over after 10 minutes.

16 Cool the baps on a wire rack.

CHEESE SCONES

I prefer to use 81% wheatmeal flour in this recipe because it is slightly lighter than wholemeal. These little scones rise beautifully and won't last very long on the cooling rack, so I advise you to make double the quantity in the recipe if you want to have enough left for the tea table!

The recipe makes ten scones.

Equipment	Ingredients
A mixing bowl	8 oz (225g) 81% wholemeal flour *or* 4 oz (115g) each of wholemeal and unbleached white flour
A sieve	
A rolling pin	
A 2-inch (5cm) round pastry cutter	2 slightly rounded teaspoons baking powder
A wire rack	¼ teaspoon sea salt
A large baking tray, greased and floured	½ teaspoon mustard powder
A pastry brush	1½ oz (45g) polyunsaturated margarine
	3 oz (85g) finely grated Cheddar cheese
Pre-heat the oven to 425°F (220°C/Gas Mark 7)	¼ pint (140ml) natural yogurt
	A little milk

1 Sieve the flour, baking powder, sea salt and mustard powder into the mixing bowl.

2 Rub in the margarine until the mixture looks like very fine crumbs.

3 Add the cheese, blending lightly to prevent lumps forming.

4 Make a well in the middle and pour in the yogurt.

5 Form into a soft dough with your hands. Knead in the bowl for a few seconds.

6 Roll out on a lightly-floured surface to a thickness of ½ inch (1cm).

7 Cut into rounds and place on the baking tray.

8 Brush the tops with milk and sprinkle on a little flour.

9 Bake for 12 minutes until the tops are golden-brown and the scones are well risen.

10 Cool on a wire rack.

FRUITY DROP SCONES

Plain drop scones are very nice if they are served warm, spread with a little butter or margarine but these fruit scones make a pleasant change. If you want to make traditional drop scones, just leave out the fruit and spice and follow the instructions for mixing and cooking below.

Equipment
A liquidizer or a food
   processor, *or* a mixing bowl,
   a fork and a sieve
A non-stick frying pan
An old pastry brush
A pallet knife
A saucer for oil
A tablespoon

Ingredients
10 dried apricot halves
Apple juice for soaking
   apricots
8 oz (225g) wholemeal flour
1½ teaspoons baking powder
½ teaspoon cinnamon *or*
   mixed spice
1 egg
½ pint (275ml) milk
1 teaspoon clear honey
1 tablespoon sunflower oil for
   frying

1 Wash the apricots in boiling water, drain and cover with apple juice. Soak for 2 hours.

2 Drain the apricots (keep the juice for drinking) and chop them into very small pieces.

3 If you have a mixer, blend the chopped apricots and all the other ingredients, except the oil, until the mixture is smooth.

4 If mixing by hand, sieve the flour, baking powder and spice into the bowl.

5 Make a well in the centre and add the egg and half the milk. Mix with a fork to a smooth paste.

6 Gradually add the rest of the milk to make a thickish batter.

7 Stir in the apricots and honey. (You can sieve the apricots for a smoother texture and sweeter taste.)

8 Brush the pan with oil and put on medium heat. When the oil is hot, drop tablespoonfuls of the batter into the pan (about three at a time) and cook until the top is covered with bubbles. Flip them over with a pallet knife and cook on the other side for 30 seconds. Keep the scones warm in a clean folded cloth.

SWEETHEART CAROB CAKE

This is a chocolate cake without the chocolate! I use carob powder instead of cocoa in this recipe because cocoa contains caffeine which is bad for you. Carob powder, which comes from the seeds of the locust tree, tastes like chocolate, is naturally sweet, is much cheaper then cocoa, and has no caffeine in it. So try using carob, not only in this recipe, but in other recipes where cocoa is listed in the ingredients. I'll bet you that no one will spot the difference unless you tell them.

Equipment
A 9-inch (23cm) diameter
   heart-shaped cake tin,
   greased and lined
3 medium-sized bowls
A small bowl
A wooden spoon
A fork
An egg whisk
A small saucepan
A heatproof plate
A wire rack

Pre-heat the oven to 350°F
   (180°C/Gas Mark 4)

Ingredients

For the cake
8 oz (225g) wholemeal self-
   raising flour
1 oz (30g) carob powder
2 oz (55g) ground almonds
8 oz (225g) polyunsaturated
   margarine
8 oz (225g) clear honey
A few drops of vanilla essence
4 large eggs

For the topping
3 oz (85g) carob confectioner's
   bar (slightly sweetened)
1 tablespoon thick natural
   yogurt
1 tablespoon double dream
1 teaspoon finely grated
   orange peel
1½ oz (45g) chopped and
   toasted hazelnuts (optional)

For the cake

1 Sieve the flour, carob and almonds into a bowl.

2 Cream the margarine and honey in another bowl for 1 minute only.

3 Separate the eggs. Put the yolks into the small bowl and whisk lightly with a fork. Put the egg whites into a medium-sized bowl.

4 Add a few drops of vanilla essence to the yolks and beat into the margarine and honey.

5 Gradually add the flour mixture, folding it in gently (do not beat).

6 Whisk the egg whites until stiff and fold into the mixture (do not beat).

7 Spoon into the prepared tin and bake in the centre of the oven for 1 hour.

8 Leave the cake in the tin for 5 minutes, then cool on a wire rack. Let it get completely cold before topping.

For the topping

1 Half fill the saucepan with water and bring to the boil. Turn down to simmer.

2 Put the heatproof plate on top. Break up the carob bar and put the pieces on the plate to melt.

3 Whisk the cream in a small bowl. Stir in the yogurt and the melted carob.

4 When the cake is quite cold, spread this mixture over the top.

5 If you have the hazelnuts, sprinkle them all over the top or in a thick band around the edge. Keep the cake in a cool place.

If you want some more decoration, you can put crystallized violets around the edge, or all over the top with the hazelnuts.

CAROB BIRTHDAY CAKE

Use a round 9 inch (23cm) instead of a heart-shaped one. Follow the directions for the Sweetheart cake, but make double the topping.

When the cake is cool, cut it in half horizontally. Spread 2 tablespoons no-sugar strawberry or raspberry jam and half the carob cream in the centre, sandwich the two halves together and spread the rest of the cream on top of the cake. Decorate with a band of chopped hazelnuts and of course candles.

EASY APPLE PIE

Equipment	Ingredients
A 9 inch (22cm) pie dish, about 2 inch (5cm) deep, greased	3 large cooking apples, cored and sliced (leave skins on)
A small saucepan	2 tablespoons clear honey
Foil	½ teaspoon ground cinnamon
A rolling pin	¼ teaspoon ground clove powder
A palette knife	1 oz (30g) polyunsaturated margarine
A pastry brush	1 quantity of sweet shortcrust pastry (see page 71)
A fork	1 teaspoon demerara sugar for topping (optional)
Pre-heat the oven to 400°F (200°C/Gas Mark 6)	A little milk to brush the top

1 Layer the apple slices in the pie dish.

2 Put the honey in the saucepan with the spices and heat very gently for 30 seconds until the honey is very runny.

3 Trickle the honey and spices over the apples and dot with the margarine.

4 Cover the dish with foil and bake for 15 minutes, until the apples are fairly soft. Leave to cool.

5 Roll out the chilled pastry on a lightly-floured surface. Flatten it to a circle a bit larger then the dish

6 Ease the pastry from the work surface with the palette knife and lift it onto the rolling pin. Curl it up a little as you lift and place it on top of the cooled apples. Trim off the edges and save the trimmings.

7 Mark the edges with a fork, or pinch them with your fingers to make a fluted border.

8 Press the trimmings together and roll out to ¼ inch (½ cm) thick and cut out leaf shapes to decorate the centre of the pie (see diagram).

9 Brush the underside of the leaf shapes with milk and put them on the pie. Then brush the whole surface of the pie with milk. Sprinkle on a little sugar if you wish.

10 Prick the pastry with a fork and bake the pie in the oven for 25 minutes.

SESAME COOKIES

This recipe makes twenty-five cookies, which may sound a lot, but they are so good that you will be lucky if you manage to put some in the tin for another day. Do not use baking powder instead of bicarbonate of soda, or the cookies will not be crisp and crunchy.

Equipment
2 baking trays, greased and
    sprinkled with a few
    sesame seeds (you will use
    these twice)
A cup and a teaspoon
A mixing bowl
A wooden spoon
A small saucepan
A wire rack
Pre-heat the oven to 325°F
    (160°F/Gas Mark 3)

Ingredients
2 level teaspoons bicarbonate
    of soda
1 tablespoon hot water
4 oz (115g) polyunsaturated
    margarine
1 generous tablespoon malt
    extract (about 3 oz/85g)
3 oz (85g) demerara sugar
3 oz (85g) sesame seeds
4 oz (115g) wholemeal flour
3 oz (85g) porridge oats

1 Mix the bicarbonate of soda and the hot water together in the cup.

2 Put the margarine, malt and sugar in the saucepan and melt on very low heat (do not boil).

3 Mix the sugar, seeds, flour and oats in the mixing bowl.

4 Pour in the malt and bicarbonate of soda liquids and blend all the ingredients together.

5 Roll the mixture into small balls, (about 1 inch (2½cm) in diameter), and spread these out on the trays. You will have to do two batches (two trays at a time).

6 Place the trays in the oven, one just above the centre and the other just below, and bake for 20 minutes. Change the trays around after 10 minutes.

7 Cool on the trays for 5 minutes, then leave them on a wire rack until they are cold. Store in a tin or airtight container.

COCONUT COOKIES

Follow all the directions for sesame cookies but leave out the sesame seeds and add 3 oz (85g) desiccated coconut.

GINGERBREAD PEOPLE

These are great for parties. You can put them in little polythene bags tied with a bow and give them to your guests as a parting gift. Another idea is to decorate your birthday cake with them. All you do is stand them up around the edge and secure them with a thin ribbon. They are a bit fiddly to make so it is a good idea to bake them the day before, leave them to cool and then put them in an airtight tin until you need them.

Equipment	Ingredients
2 large baking trays, greased	8 oz (25g) fine wholemeal
Gingerbread-men cutters	pastry flour
A mixing bowl	1 level teaspoon baking
A medium-sized bowl	powder
A sieve	1 slightly rounded teaspoon
A wooden spoon	ground ginger
A rolling pin	½ level teaspoon bicarbonate
A palette knife	of soda
	3 oz (85g) polyunsaturated
	margarine
	3 oz (85g) soft brown sugar
	3 oz (85g) raw cane syrup
Pre-heat the oven to 400°F	A few currants and glacé
(200°C/Gas Mark 6)	cherries to decorate

1 Sieve the flour, baking powder and bicarbonate of soda into the medium-sized bowl.

2 Cream the margarine, sugar and syrup until light and fluffy.

3 Stir in the flour mixture, kneading with your hands to work well in.

4 Leave the dough in a polythene bag for 30 minutes before rolling out.

5 Roll out the dough on a lightly-floured surface to about ¼ inch (½ cm) thick. Cut out the figures and lift them on to the baking trays.

6 Press currants into each figure for eyes and buttons, and add a little sliver of cherry for the mouth.

7 Bake one tray at a time in the centre of the oven for 10 minutes.

8 Cool the gingerbread figures on the tray and allow them to harden before storing in an airtight container.

6. SOME TASTY EXTRAS

ALL-DAY CRUNCHY BITE GRANOLA

Granola is a mixture of toasted wholegrains, nuts and seeds which you can have for breakfast with dried or fresh fruit, milk or yogurt. But if you like nibbling at snacks throughout the day, try the mixture in this recipe. It's tasty and crunchy, and far better for you than a bar of chocolate.

Equipment	Ingredients
A medium-sized baking tray	2 oz (55g) hazelnuts
A large baking tray	2 oz (55g) sesame seeds
A mixing bowl	2 oz (55g) sunflower seeds
A small saucepan	8 oz (225g) porridge oats
A fork	1 oz (30g) wheatgerm
A screw-top jar	(optional)
	1 tablespoon malt extract
	1 tablespoon clear honey
	2 tablespoons corn oil or
	sunflower oil
	A good pinch of sea salt
Pre-heat the oven to 375°F (190°C/Gas Mark 3)	4 oz (115g) raisins or sultanas

1 Put the nuts and seeds onto the medium-sized baking tray and toast them in the oven for 15 minutes until lightly browned.

2 While these are toasting, put the oats, wheatgerm and salt into the mixing bowl.

3 Put the honey, malt and oil into the saucepan and melt on low heat until the mixture will pour easily. Be careful not to burn it.

4 Trickle the malt liquid into the oat mixture and stir it in well with a fork.

5 Rub the mixture between your fingers until it is like rough bread-crumbs.

6 Spread this out on the large baking tray.

7 Take out the nuts when they are ready.

8 Turn down the oven to 300°F (150°C/Gas Mark 2) and bake the oat and malt mixture for 40 minutes. Turn the mixture over with a fork every 15 minutes so that it browns evenly.

9 Mix the oat mixture with the nuts, seeds and raisins. Leave to cool and then store in a large screw-top jar. Nibble some whenever you have the urge for a bar of chocolate and you will fill that hungry gap with something sweet and nourishing.

POPCORN HONEY MUNCH

Here is another crunchy snack which is fun to make. You can eat the popcorn straight from the pot with just a pinch of sea salt to give a savoury taste, or try this tasty idea of coating it with malt and honey and toasting it in the oven until it is crisp. Young children love a bag of popcorn as a going-home gift after a party — or you can put some in small polythene bag, tie them with pretty ribbons and hang them on the Christmas tree.

Equipment	Ingredients
A large, heavy-based saucepan with a lid	3 oz (85g) popping corn
A small saucepan	1 level tablespoon malt extract (heat the spoon in hot water. This will melt the malt and make it easy to level out.)
A fork	
A large baking tray, well greased	
A screw-top jar	2 tablespoons polyunsaturated margarine
	A pinch of sea salt (optional)
Pre-heat the oven to 350°F (180°C/Gas Mark 4)	

1 Warm the saucepan on medium heat.

2 Keep the pan on medium heat and add the popcorn. Wait until you hear the first pop, then put the lid on the pan until the corn has finished popping. Shake the pan well and often during popping time.

3 When the popping stops, take the pan off the heat. Leave it to cool for a minute or two, then take out any unpopped corn.

4 Heat the honey, malt, oil and salt in the small saucepan. Be careful not to burn it.

5 Stir this mixture into the popped corn, coating it well.

6 Spread the corn out evenly on the baking tray and bake in the centre of the oven for 15 minutes.

7 Cool the popcorn on the tray. It will get crisp as it cools. Store in a screw-top jar or any airtight container.

FRUIT AND NUT SNOWBALLS

The ingredients used in this recipe are very similar to those in the expensive fruit bars you can buy in health food stores. You can make your own bars by forming the mixture into rectangle shapes, and wrapping them in cellophane paper, and storing them in a tin ready for a lunch-box treat. Here, the mixture is formed into small balls and rolled in coconut. They make a nice simple gift if you put them into little coloured boxes and tie them with silver string.

Equipment	Ingredients
A hand or electric mincer	6 oz (175g) stoned dates
A mixing bowl	4 oz (115g) dried apricots
A plastic box with lid	4 oz (115g) raisins
	6 oz (175g) mixed nuts and
	sunflower seeds
	1 oz (30g) desiccated coconut

1 Wash the apricots by pouring boiling water over them. Pat them dry with a clean cloth.

2 Mix all the fruit, nuts and seeds in a bowl and mince the mixture a handful at a time.

3 Thoroughly mould the minced ingredients with your hands for 1 minute.

4 Rinse your hands and form the mixture into small balls. Roll these in the coconut coating.

5 Store in a plastic box between layers of greaseproof paper. Cover the box with a tight lid and keep in the fridge.

BANANAMAL ICE POPS

You can buy small animal-shaped moulds to freeze but you can't find any of these, an ordinary ice lolly tray will do.

These pops are really refreshing on hot summer days and far better for you than shop ice lollies which are usually full of colourings and flavourings and rarely have any fruit in them.

Equipment	Ingredients
A fork	2 medium-sized bananas
A mixing bowl	8 oz (225g) natural yogurt
An animal-shaped mould or	1 teaspoon fresh lemon juice
ordinary ice lolly tray	2 teaspoons clear honey

1 Mash the bananas.

2 Blend all the ingredients together in the bowl, spoon into the moulds and freeze.

Variation

Use other fruits instead of bananas. For example, fresh strawberries are cheap in July. One punnet (about 6 oz/170g) will be enough. All you do is wash the berries and press them through a sieve. Leave out the lemon juice and mix the strawberry purée with the honey and yogurt. Taste and add a little more honey if you like. Strawberry pops are deliciously cooling.

APPENDIX: COOKING AIDS FOR THE HANDICAPPED AND THE VERY YOUNG

The bits and pieces described here have enabled lots of handicapped children to take up cookery. They are also very valuable in helping the frustrated little ones get going sooner. They can all be made very easily from oddments of wood and scrap materials held together with drawing pins, nails and glue. If you literally can't knock a nail in straight and you do not have a friendly do-it-yourself fanatic living next door, then try asking your local comprehensive school craft department to help.

Designed and illustrated by Eric Birchell.

HAND HELD VEG'GRIPPER

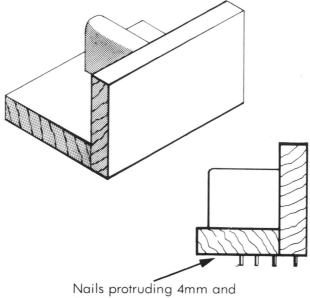

Nails protruding 4mm and flattened.

HAND PROTECTOR

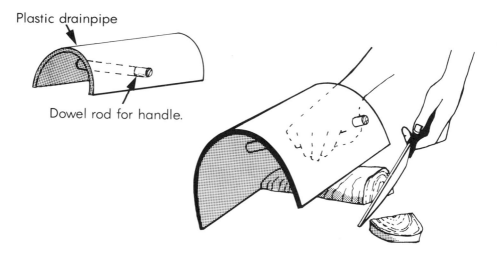

Plastic drainpipe

Dowel rod for handle.

VEG GRIPPER   For peeling, grating, chipping.

Teeth sawn in

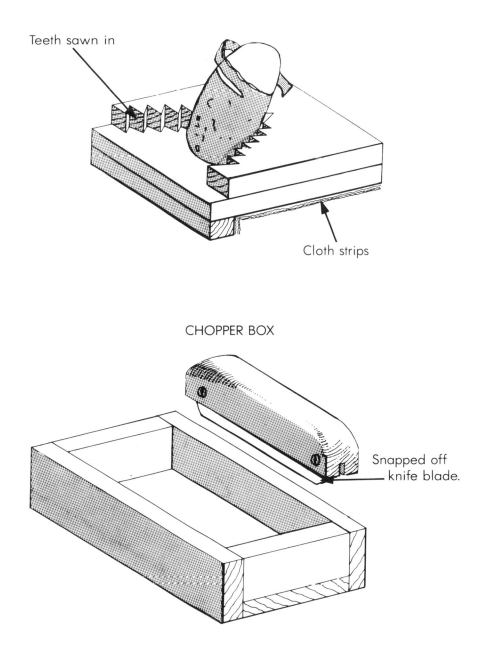

Cloth strips

CHOPPER BOX

Snapped off
knife blade.

INDEX